ID0940879

The Calling

A Journey Within Your Own Being

by
Steven S. Sadleir

The Calling

A Journey Within Your Own Being

by
Steven S. Sadleir

Self Awareness Institute Publishing
219 Broadway, Suite 417, Laguna Beach, CA 92461

The Calling
A Journey Within Your Own Being

Published by:
The Self Awareness Institute
219 Broadway, Suite 417, Laguna Beach, CA 92651
(714) 491-3356

Distributed by: BookPeople in Oakland, Ca
and New Leaf in Atlanta, Ga

c. Copyright 1994 Steven S. Sadleir. All rights reserved.
No part of this book may be reproduced by any means without
written permission of the publisher. Please feel free to quote
liberally and include the name of author and title.

ISBN 1-883544-02-5

First Printing March 1995

The mandala used on the cover The Blossoming of the Soul
was painted by Paul Heussenstamm (714) 497-2708
P.O. Box 836, Laguna Beach, CA 92652

Dedication

This book is dedicated to that which is calling
you to read it.

Acknowledgements

Thank you Maureen Maher and Katy Bonnett for editing the manuscript, Paul Heussenstamm for the beautiful mandala painting that is on the book jacket, Regina Rolland for computer wizardry, friends at SAJ for the encouragement to write this book, and God for the inspiration to write it.

Preface

Take a deep breath, sit back and relax. You are about to embark on a journey within your own being. You are being called to wake up from the dream – to remember who you are and why you were born – so that you may fulfill your life's purpose. Your awakening has already begun; you have been called to read this. That which is compelling you to read on will continue to guide you to full self realization.

Take your time with each thought to contemplate its meaning at greater depth. You will naturally undergo subtle shifts in awareness as you are reading, and you will likely space out at times as your awareness transcends mental cognitive processes. Give yourself these moments without the burden of having to understand. Your intuition will guide you to flashes of insight, and understanding will naturally develop, like a picture forming within your own mind.

It is no coincidence that you are reading these words at this particular time in your life.

You have come to a pivotal point in the evolution of your consciousness where you are ready to fully remember who you are and what your purpose in life is.

A part of you already knows this.

Acknowledge that part of you that
senses that it is ready to evolve itself
further, and wants to awaken.

Observe your impetus to read on.

Your consciousness is calling you to wake up from the dream and fulfill the purpose for which you incarnated.

4

In order to fulfill your life purpose, you must first be conscious of the Self that has a purpose to fulfill.

The part of you that is aware of itself is the Self.

The part of you that can reflect upon the meaning of these words is your consciousness.

The more conscious you are of your consciousness, the more your consciousness evolves.

As you evolve your consciousness, you become more aware of your Self and its purpose.

In this moment, as you reflect upon what it means to be conscious, you are evolving your conscious awareness.

It is your higher consciousness that is compelling you to read on, so that you can fulfill the purpose of your existence.

Your destiny is unfolding as you begin to realize the significance of what this means.

Realizing that there is a Self to be realized invokes that realization.

Having considered this, your realization has begun.

The more that you reflect on this, the greater your realization.

The part of you that knows who you are
and why you were born is making
conscious contact with you now through
these words.

As you consider how this could be, the part of you which is considering it is becoming conscious of itself.

Observe what is occurring within you in this moment.

*N*ow observe the part of you that is observing.

Observe the observer observing the observing.

Your consciousness is reflecting upon itself.

19

As your consciousness reflects upon itself, you are seeing yourself for what you are.

You are the consciousness.

When the body and mind expire, consciousness is all that remains.

Recognize this consciousness within you, and see your body and mind as a vehicle for its expression.

Similar to how you come to know your appearance by seeing it reflected back to you, you come to know your own nature by reflecting upon your own nature.

Reflect on your own nature.

*N*ow reflect on your ability to reflect upon your own nature.

As you reflect upon what this means, what part of you is able to observe this self reflection?

Observe your ability to be conscious.

Thinking about your own nature makes you more conscious.

The more conscious you become, the less unconscious you are.

With greater conscious awareness come greater clarity, insight, happiness and peace.

The more disconnected we are with our consciousness, the more we feel disconnected and are less happy and fulfilled in life.

You are either conscious or unconscious. Who decides what state you are going to be in?

Who is the you who is considering what all this means?

Reflecting upon the meaning of who you are places a mental mirror up to your own nature.

Ask your Self "who am I?"

Ask your Self "who am I" again, and listen to the answer within the quiet of your own mind.

Who am I ?

*N*ow enquire into the nature of the one
asking itself the question.

From where does the volition come for you to reflect upon this meaning?

What are you feeling as you reflect on this?

Who is observing this feeling?

*W*here does this feeling come from?

Follow this feeling back to its source.

Think about what you are thinking about in this moment.

Observe your mind as you watch thoughts arise.

Follow your thoughts back to their source.

Go back to the quiet place before thoughts arise.

Observe the places between your thoughts.

Who is observing non-thought?

As you are reading these words light is reflecting off the page and entering into your eyes, sending a signal to your brain.

Observe this.

Your brain is relating current visual signals to past imprints of written material and assigning a meaning to the imprints which we call words.

Observe this.

As you think about this, energy is traveling through fields of neurons in your brain – Like wind blowing across the surface of water creating ripples of thought.

Observe this.

*Y*our understanding is the relationship between the points along this wave of thought which forms an image in your mind.

*W*ho is reflecting upon this thought?

*O*bserve this.

What part of you can discern if you understand this or not?

Observe this.

What part of you desires to understand this?

Where does this impetus to understand come from?

Who's longing to know?

Surrender the effort of trying to understand, and observe what remains.

Observe how your thoughts obscure
what is.

All that we are just is as it is, and it is only our perception of what is that ever changes.

Surrender all that you think that you are and perceive yourself to be, and observe what remains.

Your true Self is already realized; only your mind creates the sense of having to remember or attain a realization.

Surrender your mental effort of trying to understand or realize your true nature and you can just be as you are.

You already are that which you are.

The essence of what you are is related through the sense of being.

Being is reflected through your consciousness.

You have never known not being; your consciousness gives you a sense of Self.

Your individual consciousness is wholly a part of the whole consciousness which underlies everything that you are conscious of.

Individual consciousness only appears separate when your mind reflects on it.

Your mind is but a movement of consciousness.

When the mind is still, you are fully conscious.

Your consciousness is like a blackboard, with all the space interconnected as one infinite whole.

The point of reference that you think of as your individual self is like the point at the end of a piece of chalk.

Your mind is the movement of chalk across the blackboard.

As your mind projects thought, it leaves a trail of reference points that takes the form of appearances.

Your sense of individual self
distinguishes you from the wholeness
like a chalk point on a blackboard.

As you draw lines with your mind, your
awareness is contracted to a linear
perspective and time and space appear to
occur.

63

As pictures are drawn with your mind, the contrast between the light and dark creates a subject-object relationship and differentiation appears to occur.

The chalk is still only covering the blackboard with appearances.

No matter where you put the chalk, the blackboard is there providing for its appearance.

Appearances come and go, but the blackboard remains the same.

The consciousness remains complete and whole, regardless of what is projected on it through the mind.

If you stop drawing pictures with your mind for a moment and step back from the blackboard, you will behold the interconnected wholeness of your own being.

You are the blackboard.

You are the chalk, and the one drawing with the chalk.

You are the movement of the chalk, the picture that it forms, and the one beholding the drawing that you created.

Thoughts are projected upon a screen of emptiness within your mind. Before thought, after thought, around thought and within thought is emptiness. Observe that emptiness.

Like ripples across a pond, the mind disrupts your ability to reflect upon the whole.

$\mathcal{A}$s the mind becomes still, like a placid lake, it reflects back to you your own nature – the whole of your being.

The clearer your mind becomes, the greater clarity you develop.

Without the confinement of your awareness to that which your mind is projecting, your consciousness is unbounded, liberated, ecstatic.

The more you look for, acknowledge and express your consciousness, the more you evolve your consciousness and develop greater Self awareness.

The more that you see the consciousness being reflected back to you through all that you experience, the more your individual consciousness integrates into the universal consciousness.

As you become increasingly more conscious of how your individual consciousness works in concert with the universal consciousness, you will see how the consciousness is directing and guiding you through your whole life experience.

The more conscious you become of how the consciousness is guiding you, the more you will be consciously guided.

The more that you are consciously guided, the more you fulfill your life's purpose and live in happiness and peace.

As you attune to this guiding influence, you live in harmony and balance.

To the degree that you are not tuning in to this guidance, you feel discord and out of balance.

When you act unconsciously you restrict the flow of consciousness being expressed. This creates a friction that is felt as resistance, and your life experiences become increasingly more difficult in order to indicate where your blockages are.

As you surrender your resistances your consciousness will guide you and your life will flow more smoothly.

To the degree that you are open to receive this intuitive guidance, you will receive it.

Your whole life experience is providing lessons for you to evolve in awareness and fulfill your life purpose.

Everything that you experience is teaching you something about your Self.

The more that you see this, the more that you will awaken and will not have to create difficult lessons to snap yourself back into being more conscious.

When you are conscious, there is clarity, happiness and peace - even bliss.

Therefore, any time that you are feeling anything other than clarity, happiness and peace, it is only serving as a reminder to become conscious again.

As you evolve greater clarity, happiness and peace in your life, you are in a better position to share this awareness with others.

The more that you share consciously with others, the more conscious those with whom you are sharing with become, and you will feel more fulfilled for sharing yourself with others. Life has more meaning when you give more of your Self.

The more that individuals become conscious, the more conscious the world becomes.

Conscious people don't hurt one another, pollute the environment, destroy valuable resources, procreate indiscriminately, place monetary values above human values, lie, cheat, deceive, or disrespect others. These are the result of unconscious acts.

Conscious people are conscientious, compassionate and kind. The nature of consciousness is loving and peaceful.

We all have this intrinsic higher nature; once we recognize it we can utilize it.

You can bring it out in others who are not conscious of it, by recognizing it within them and by helping them to recognize it within themselves.

Those who don't see it are the ones who need it invoked within them the most. For the sake of the whole, we must invoke the consciousness within each part of the whole to live happily and peacefully as one whole.

Each individual consciousness is like a cell in the body of God. If one cell is infected, it can infect the whole organism; as individual cells heal this invokes a healing that serves as a catalyst to heal the collective consciousness of humanity. As you awaken, the world awakens.

Other parts of the whole are destroying themselves. Like a cancer, human beings are hurting themselves and others through unconscious thinking and acting.
Those who are aware of being one with the whole must work to heal each part of themselves, so that we may all live together in happiness and peace.

We create a happy and peaceful world through the collective efforts of each individual making the effort to create happiness and peace in their own world, and then sharing that love with everyone they see, everywhere they go, all the time, every day.

Imagine a world where we all lived together in happiness and peace.

What would that look like?

What would your world look like if you were creating happiness and peace within the world that you live?

What steps could you make to create complete happiness and peace in your life?

Where does happiness and peace come from? Where are you looking?

*W*hat could you do to create greater happiness and peace in this world?

*A*ssume that you can make a difference, and now look for the opportunities in your life to make your contribution.

To the degree that you extend yourself, you create a greater capacity for higher consciousness to be expressed through all that you think, say and do.

The more the consciousness is expressed, the more conscious you are. The more you live your life consciously, the more you fulfill your life purpose and live in happiness and peace.

You are being guided through your life experience.

Look for the signs and opportunities to share your awareness with others.

Observe the coincidences that come up in your life, follow your intuition, and go with what feels right in your heart.

The more conscious you are, the clearer your course of action is.

Be quiet. Don't do anything. Don't try and don't not try. Just be and all will be clear to you.

The part of you that can observe your mind already has perfect clarity. Your Self is guiding you. Step out of your own way. Just be.

You are that which is calling you.

105

By contemplating these thoughts you
have invoked them into your awareness.

You have awakened from the dream.
All thoughts and activities arise within
the infinite depths of your being. You are
the beingness.

Nothing else needs to happen. There is nothing you need to do. That which is, already is as it is. You already are that which you are. Realize it.

Take all that you have just read and let it go. Give up all that you think you understand and don't understand.

Surrender the effort of trying to know, and the one who is trying.

Just be; you are free.

About the Author

Steven Sadleir has been involved with Yoga and meditation since childhood and has studied with several spiritual masters, including Vethathiri Maharishi and Shivabalayogi Maharaj, with whom he received his training as a yogi. He is a native of Southern California, holds a Masters Degree in Economics, and worked in finance for several years. He now devotes himself full time to helping others awaken by teaching at the Self Awareness Institute, which he founded in 1989. Steve is also author of *The Spiritual Seeker's Guide, The Complete Source for Religions and Spiritual Groups of the World*, and *The Awakening, An Evolutionary Leap in Human Consciousness*.

Books by Steven S. Sadleir

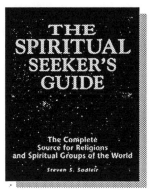

The Spiritual Seeker's Guide by Steven S. Sadleir is a who's who of all the major spiritual paths and teachers of the world, including Eastern and Western religions, occult teachings, mystery schools and shamanistic paths, new age teachings, channels and spiritual masters of the world complete with photographs, addresses and phone numbers. The most complete unbiased synopsis of world spiritual traditions available.

ISBN 1-880741-28-8 $15.00 inclusive

"Amazingly thorough"   —Yoga Journal

You are in the midst of an awakening, and are being guided to fulfill your life purpose. The Awakening by Steven S. Sadleir provides you tools that will unlock your innate potential and fulfill your life purpose. It contains valuable meditation tools to develop greater awareness.

ISBN 1-883544-00-9 $15.00 inclusive

"A beautiful book, full of profundity and sensitivity"
—Ram Dass

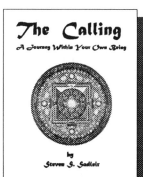

NEW!

The Calling, a Journey Within Your Own Being by Steven S. Sadleir IS a meditation. As you are reading this book you will undergo a shift in your conscious awareness as it is being explained to you. Recommended for the advanced inner traveler.

ISBN 1-883544-02-5 $15.00 inclusive

Order through your bookstore or by mail.   Send check or money order to:

Spiritual Seeker's Guide _____ @ $15.00_____
The Awakening _____ @ $15.00_____   The Self Awareness Institute
The Calling _____ @ $15.00_____   219 Broadway, Suite 417
                                                  Laguna Beach, CA 92651
Please ship to:
Name:_____
Address:_____
C/S/Z _____
Phone_____

Guided Meditation Cassette Tapes

by Steven S. Sadleir

**Each cassette provides you a different tool
for developing greater awareness.
Each tape is $10.00 inclusive.**

Tape 1—**The Third Eye** - This takes you through a transformative journey through different states of consciousness. 30 min. Second side is a guided relaxation /healing exercise.

Tape 2—**The Power of Breath** - This active meditation brings your awareness together with the prana or life force energy with the effect of transcending body-mind consciousness. Side two helps release blockages in the navel, heart and mind to help open you to that which already is.

Tape 3—**The Mind Mirror** - This cassette takes you on a walk within your own mind to reveal your own higher consciousness. Side two exposes the listeners to deeper aspects of themselves.

Tape 4—**The Calling, A Journey Within Your Own Being** - Here you are guided through a gateway and into higher consciousness as you are listening to the tape. For advanced meditators.

THE
SELF
AWARENESS
INSTITUTE

MEDITATIONS
AND DISCOURSES
by
STEVEN S. SADLEIR

Order through your bookstore or by mail.

Tape #1 _____ @ $10.00 _____
Tape #2 _____ @ $10.00 _____
Tape #3 _____ @ $10.00 _____
Tape #4 _____ @ $10.00 _____

Send check or money order to:
    The Self Awareness Institute
    219 Broadway, Suite 417
    Laguna Beach, CA 92651
Please ship to:

Name:_____

Address: _____

C/S/Z _____

Phone _____

Do you ever feel like there must be something more to life?

There Is!...

Deep inside there is a part of you that knows what your calling in life is. All you need to do is access it, and all it takes is the right tools and training.

Our answers lie within us, but in a place that we are not accustomed to looking. Over 90% of your brain potential is inactive. In our Awareness Intensives we teach you how to awaken your faculties of higher awareness and develop your intuitive guidance.

Programs are periodically held at our center in Laguna Beach, California and all over the world. To receive a FREE newsletter with schedule of upcoming events just write us at:

The Self Awareness Institute
219 Broadway, Suite 417
Laguna Beach, CA 92651
(714) 491-3356

You Can Help

Word of mouth is the best way for us to get the word out. You could really help us by telling your friends about this book and by asking your local bookstore and library to carry it. Thank you.